Feeling for Others

Caring for Others

Dalton Blaine

SOCIAL AND EMOTIONAL LEARNING FOR THE REAL WORLD™

Rosen Classroom™

You can care for others.

What do they feel?
Try to help.

Your friend is sad.
Make them smile.

Give a hug.
Hold their hand.

Your sister is scared.
Listen to her.

Stay with her.
Bring a flashlight!

Your teacher is sick.
Show you care.

Give a card.
Give balloons.

Care for friends.
Care for family.

Care for everyone.
Be kind!

Words to Know

balloon

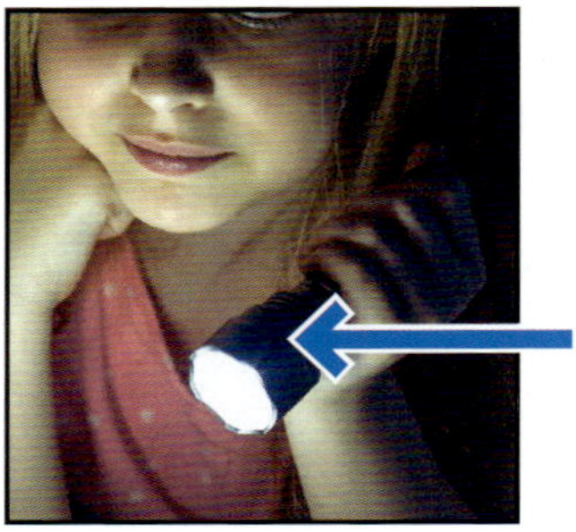

flashlight

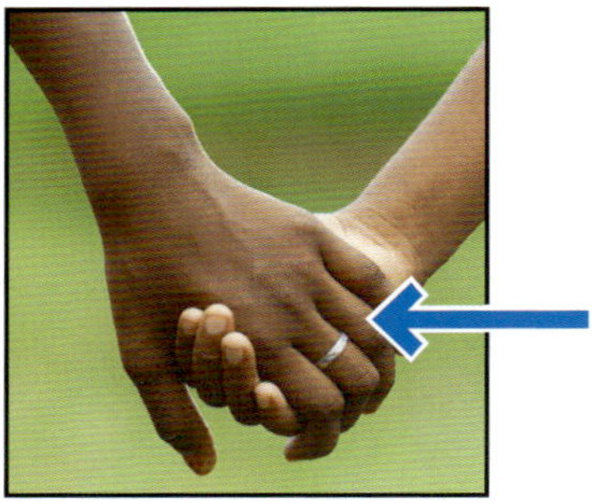

hand